The ARTS

DANCE

Eleanor Van Zandt

STECK-VAUGHN
L I B R A R Y
Austin, Texas

The Arts

Architecture
Dance
Design
Literature
The Movies
Music
Painting and Sculpture
Photography
Theater

Cover illustration: Dancer Wayne Sleep on stage
with other dancers from *The Hot Shoe Show*

Series and Book Editor: Rosemary Ashley
Designer: David Armitage
Consultant: June Layson PhD,
Director of Dance Studies,
University of Surrey, Guildford, England

**Published in the United States in 1990 by Steck-Vaughn
Co., Austin, Texas,** a subsidiary of National Education
Corporation.

First published in 1988 by Wayland (Publishers) Limited

Library of Congress Cataloging-in-Publication Data

Van Zandt, Eleanor.
  Dance.

  (The Arts)
  Includes bibliographical references.
  Summary: Surveys dance as an art form, examining
such categories as folk dance, ballet, modern dance,
ballroom dancing, and contemporary dance, and
discussing the creation and recording of dance.
  1. Dancing—Juvenile literature.   2. Dancing—
History—Juvenile literature. [1. Dancing]   I. Title.
II. Series: Arts (Austin, Tex.)
GV1596.5.V36   1990   792.8   89-21723
ISBN 0-8114-2357-3

Printed in Italy
Bound in the United States
1 2 3 4 5 6 7 8 9 0 Sa 94 93 92 91 90

Contents

1 The Oldest Art

Dance is probably the oldest of all the arts. Certainly it is the most instinctive. We only need to watch a baby in its crib, waving and beating its arms and legs, apparently for sheer pleasure, to realize how basic is the human delight in rhythmic movement.

From such simple movements, many thousands of years ago, dance must have developed. We cannot trace its development with any certainty; but from studying the dances of ancient cultures today, we can guess that in most of them dance began with spontaneous stamping movements. Later, these movements were formalized into various rhythms and patterns, often involving the whole community. Music to accompany dance would have consisted originally of grunts or cries. Then simple musical instruments such as drums and pipes were devised in order to provide a beat and a tune; but the earliest dancers provided the beat themselves. And they must have discovered early on that the repetition of a certain rhythm has amazing power. Many of these ancient dances went on for hours, with the dancers eventually working themselves into a trance, which allowed them to perform astonishing feats, such as walking over hot coals without burning their feet.

Below *A Native American performs a traditional mimetic dance, imitating a bear, at a dance festival held in New Mexico.*

Above *Dancing for entertainment: young competitors take part in a disco dance championship.*

Left *Dance is a very important aspect of life in Bali, Indonesia. Every dance tells a story, and the dancer's limbs — feet, ankles, hips — and her eyes and fingers, express a part of the story.*

Given this apparently magical quality of dance, it was natural for people to conclude that the dance itself could work magic. From being simply a form of recreation it became a means of communicating with the gods, or a way of ensuring a good harvest, a successful hunt, victory in battle, or another desired result. Such dances are still performed in isolated societies today.

In some of these, called mimetic dances, the dancers act out what they wish to happen. One dancer, for example, may wear a bearskin and imitate the movements of a bear, while the others threaten him with spears and finally mime the act of killing him.

In other ritual dances the movements do not appear mimetic but are intended to bring the dancer into mystical contact with the gods. A *shaman*, or medicine man, might get his patient to dance in order to rid the body of evil spirits. (The fact that the patient often does recover is evidence of a truth that has been rediscovered in this century: the dancing is good for the health, both physical and emotional.)

We can see then that although early dance was recreational — a natural expression of pleasure in movement and rhythm — it later developed into rituals. In our own highly technical culture we rarely think of dance in this way. We normally think of it either as recreation (and possibly as a way of keeping fit) or as something we watch other, professional, dancers perform as entertainment.

These three categories of dance however — recreation, rituals, and entertainment — are by no means self-contained. Each category overlaps into the others.

We may think, for example, that ritual dance has disappeared from the Western world. But we still engage in one form of ritual: the dance of courtship. In many societies, men and women rarely dance together in couples; yet boys and girls may enact, through dance, the process of choosing a mate. Several boys may dance around a girl, competing for her attention. Or boys and girls will circle around each other, or advance and retreat. Or one person will stand still while the other dances to impress the partner with his or her skill or gracefulness. Such dances can still be found in some Western cultures. In southern Germany and Austria, people dance the *schuhplattler*, which involves jumping and thigh-slapping by the men and demure turning movements by the women.

Even in dances that are not to do with courting explicitly, there is often a strong element of attracting the opposite sex. Think of solo flamenco dancers (both men and women), with their proud strutting and tossing of the head.

This "display" element, in a subtle, ultra-polite form, featured prominently in the dances of aristocratic Europe, right through the eighteenth century. But when the waltz arrived, early in the nineteenth century, there was less need for elegant figures. A sense of rhythm and mastery of one simple step were the only essential requirements. Physical contact became the important "courtship" element in the ballroom. Eventually it took over completely. By the middle of the

Above *The "Bamboo Dance," performed by the peoples of the Caroline Islands, in the South Pacific Ocean.*

Right *Senior ballet students rehearsing at the Royal Ballet School in London.*

twentieth century, many people's idea of dancing was simply to sway rhythmically while locked in a close embrace.

Now that couples have let go of each other again, the display element has come back. The way people dance may be primarily a response to the music, but it is also a way of making a statement (or several statements) about themselves.

Both ritualistic and recreational dances have often been developed not only as portrayals of rites, but also as entertainment. This has happened, for example, with some Indian dances traditionally performed as acts of worship to the Hindu gods. These dances are now widely performed on stage for audiences who may barely comprehend the story being portrayed but who can appreciate the extraordinary grace and vitality of the dancing.

Similarly, classical ballet, the most refined and demanding form of Western theatrical dance, originated in the social — that is, recreational — dances of the Renaissance. Today, however, many people attend ballet classes purely for exercise and recreation.

The enormous variety of dance among the different peoples of the world can barely be suggested in a book of this length. But we hope that by looking at some examples of dance as it has been performed and enjoyed all over the world, in the past and the present, you will gain a greater appreciation of the beauty and the life-enhancing qualities of this most physical of all the arts.

Above *In Brazil, a spiritual priestess of the Afro-Brazilian* Condomblé *religion dances to one of her gods.*

② Ancient Dance Traditions

Until the invention of motion pictures in the 1890s, it was impossible to make an exact record of a dance. Various systems of notation were devised to describe the steps of European court dances and ballet, from the Renaissance onward, but in most cultures dances have been passed on by demonstration from one generation to the next, and where a form of dance has died out, it has been lost to us forever.

In certain parts of the world people continue to dance in ways that may not have changed much over many centuries. Those dances performed as rituals — the main form of dance in many traditional societies — are unlikely to change significantly; for the magic will work only if the ritual is performed in the same way each time.

Although dance takes many forms around the world, certain movements and patterns reappear in widely scattered places. For example, the ring dance, in which the dancers form a circle, sometimes joining hands or linking arms, is common to many peoples. The circle is believed to have magical properties; what these may be varies from one society to another. Among the Cayapo Indians of Brazil, the appearance of the new moon is celebrated by women dancing in a circle, singing and stamping their feet with increasing excitement. Two children light fires inside and outside the circle.

The mysterious waxing and waning of the moon is also observed in the dances of many other peoples, often in a circular pattern. The movements of the sun, too, may inspire dances of a circular form. In the sun dance ceremony of the Plains Indians, which takes place during the summer solstice and lasts for four days, the dancers form a circular procession around a pole representing the sun.

Circles also appear in dances of initiation: Australian aborigines, for example, dance around a boy who has reached puberty. In some societies, dances consisting of two or more concentric circles are common.

In many tribal societies men and women are forbidden to dance together, and in some cases the opposite sex is forbidden even to watch. It is the men who perform war and hunting dances, and often the rain and medicine dances also. Women are more likely to perform dances connected with fertility. For example, in a fertility dance of the Iroquois Indians of northeastern America, three women are chosen to dance the roles of the three life-giving sisters, the spirits of sweetcorn, bean, and squash. Men's dances throughout the world tend to feature leaping and other displays of strength and stamina. Leaping is characteristic of many African dances, including the hunting dances of the Masai and the war dances of the Angoni, in which hundreds of

Below *At a festival in New Mexico, the feathers and bells on this Native American brave's costume accentuate his movement.*

Above *Young Masai warriors in Kenya demonstrate their leaping movement during a dance.*

dancers leap into the air simultaneously. Women's dances tend to feature less expansive movements, such as spinning or quiet rocking from side to side. Dancers of both sexes may dance for many hours without stopping.

There are few parts of the world today where cultures remain intact, unchanged by the influences of immigration and colonization. Many cultures have seen their arts, including their dance, altered, and sometimes even destroyed, through contact with an alien culture. Many

Top *Bolivian Indian women perform a traditional circular dance to the accompaniment of drums and pipes.*

Inset *A dancer performs the traditional classical Indian Kathakali dance. The hand and eye movements symbolize different emotions, and the dance is always performed by males in traditional costume and makeup.*

Native American tribes, however, have made a conscious effort to preserve their traditional dances. Some of these are performed privately, but others are performed before public audiences during special festivals. In some Iroquois and Navaho dances, among others, non-Native Americans are even invited to join in.

British imperialism very nearly succeeded in destroying one of the most beautiful of all dance forms, the ancient Indian classical dance called Bharata Natyam (or Dasi Attam). This dance dates back about 2,000 years and is native to southern India. It originally formed part of a Hindu drama. Based on principles in sacred writings, its techniques were passed down over the centuries from the gurus (spiritual teachers) to their pupils, mainly girls. Some of the dances were performed for the gods; others, for the enjoyment of humans. Many are based on the exploits of the god Shiva, Lord of the Dance, or express the dancer's love for him.

Partly because India's Christian (British) rulers in the nineteenth century regarded with horror the very idea of dance as worship, and partly because many of the temple dancers had by this time become prostitutes, the dance itself fell into disrepute. It was in danger of disappearing completely when, early in this century, Indian scholars and a few Western dancers started a movement to revive it. Today Bharata Batyam — along with other forms of Indian dance — is enormously popular, both in India and in the West.

Like all great art, Bharata Batyam can be appreciated on more than one level. There is the sensual level: the brilliantly colored costume and gold jewelry, the rhythmic excitement, punctuated with the jingling of bells around the dancer's ankles, and the grace of the movements. Then there is the dramatic emotional level, in those dances in which the dancer tells a story through numerous gestures and facial expressions, and — for a devout Hindu — the spiritual level. The dancer uses her whole body; there are thirteen gestures for the head, for example; seven for the chin; five for the waist; and hundreds for the hands. These hand gestures, or *mudras*, are perhaps the most beautiful aspect of the dance. The dancer's bare feet provide a rhythmic foundation, in addition to that supplied by a drummer and possibly a singer. Sometimes the dancer executes one rhythmic pattern (called a *jati*) while the drummer plays a different one — a feat that requires great skill and precision on the part of both performers.

The use of the hands, so important to Indian dance, traveled to other Far Eastern countries with the spread of Buddhism and features in the dance of many of these countries, including Bali, Cambodia, and Japan.

The dances of ancient Mediterranean civilizations, such as Egypt, Greece, and Rome, have long since vanished. We can only guess what they were like, from the representations of dancers in wall paintings, statues and reliefs, and pieces of pottery, as well as scattered references in ancient writings.

Wall paintings from Egyptian tombs and temples show a great variety of dance movements. Over the 4,000 years during which Egyptian civilization developed, its dance must have undergone many changes. We do know that throughout this time there were professional dancers who performed in the temples, and that during the Middle and New Kingdoms (c. 2100–700 BC), dancing girls entertained the pharaoh and his court at banquets. These dances involved running and leaping, high kicks, and sinuous movements of the hips — possibly similar to the movements of Middle Eastern belly dancers today. Acrobatic movements such as backbends and the splits were also performed.

We know that the Jews of ancient times danced, for there are frequent references to dance in the Bible. The Book of Samuel tells us that King David "danced before the Lord with all his might"; and the dance of Salome before King Herod is one of the most famous in history. But the lack of visual records and the subsequent dispersal of the Jews to other lands, where their dance underwent radical changes, has left us with almost no idea of what ancient Jewish dancing looked like.

The Greeks, by contrast, left innumerable images of people dancing. They leap and skip and whirl over the surface of countless plates, pots, and jugs. Homer's great poem, the *Iliad*, includes descriptions of groups of young men and girls dancing together, in circles and lines. The Spartans developed a weapon dance, the *pyrriché*, which was part of the standard training for warfare. Socrates observed that the best dancer makes the best warrior. Another Greek philosopher, Plato, stipulated

Above *An Indian girl performs the classical dance of Bharata Natyam. The hands play an important part in this dance, and each gesture has a precise meaning.*

11

that dance should be incorporated in his ideal republic, for it was useful in developing "noble, harmonious and graceful attitudes."

As in most cultures, Greek dance had religious origins. Celebrations honoring the goddess of love, Aphrodite, and the god of wine and fertility, Dionysus, included wild, frenzied dancing by both sexes. The wearing of masks by the dancers had religious significance and also gave the dancer a sense of losing his or her identity and magically taking on that of someone else, for whose actions one is not responsible — an experience familiar to those taking part in carnival celebrations today.

Dance was also used in Greek drama as early as 500 BC, making this the earliest recorded form of theatrical dance we know of. Like the other fine arts of Greece, it had its own muse, or source of inspiration, called Terpsichore. The Greek theatrical dancers developed the art of mime to a high degree, and their hand gestures were especially eloquent.

The Romans enjoyed watching performances by Greek dancers, and for a time it was the fashion for young ladies of noble birth to learn to dance, but the art never really formed a part of Roman civilization. For entertainment the Romans seemed to prefer to stage bloody contests between humans and animals.

Christian civilization, which supplanted that of pagan Rome, took a dim view of dance for different reasons. In most of the existing cultures of the ancient world — whether one of the major civilizations or not — dance was closely associated with pagan rites. Moreover, many of these rites often resulted in sexual free-for-alls — to which the Christian Church was implacably opposed. So dance itself, in effect, was considered immoral because of its association with pagan rites.

Left *The illustrations on this Greek vase show a flute player leading young dancers. They clearly indicate how the peoples of ancient Greece loved to dance.*

Nevertheless, there was a contrary view held within the Church that dance should be part of worship, and dances continued to be performed in churches throughout the Dark Ages. The Emperor Charlemagne forbade the custom early in the ninth century, but it was not until the twelfth century that the anti-dance supporters finally prevailed. For nearly 800 years, while music held an honored place in Christian worship, dance remained an outcast. It continued to flourish, of course, but only in secular (non-religious) forms.

Above *A wall painting on an ancient tomb at Thebes shows Egyptian dancing girls performing to guests of a Pharaoh.*

3 Western Folk Dance

Above *The Irish jig—a traditional Western folk dance involving intricate footwork and a straight torso.*

The folk dances of European peoples are as varied as the languages they speak. Compare the strenuous dance of Russian Cossacks, involving rapid thrusting out of one leg then another from a crouching position, with the graceful strathspey dance of the Lowland Scots, in which couples form interweaving patterns on the floor, dancing mainly on tiptoe. Or the rollicking Polish *mazurka*, with its stamping and heel-clicking steps, and the subtle footwork of the *sardana*, the traditional dance of Catalonia, in northeastern Spain.

Yet most European dances (and those of countries colonized by Europeans) share certain basic characteristics that distinguish them from non-Western forms. Perhaps the most noticeable of these is the straight torso. Unlike the people of Africa and Asia, many of whom use the hips, pelvis, and shoulders in their dances, Europeans have traditionally held the body erect and relatively still. Nor is there much use of hand gestures. Instead, the arms may be held up, as in some Greek dancing, or straight against the sides, as in an Irish jig. Or the hands of a group of dancers may be joined. There is a much greater emphasis on footwork than in non-Western dance. European dances tend to cover more ground, and often the essence of the dance is the pattern created on the ground by the steps. There is much more use of the straight leg. Whereas many African, Native American, and Asian dances emphasize contact with the ground and are performed with the knees slightly bent — and often with bare feet — Europeans tend to use the floor as a point of departure; although many dances acknowledge the ground with tapping or stamping, these steps are less important than kicking, jumping, and skipping.

There are plenty of exceptions to these generalizations. But in the exceptions we often find traces of non-European cultures. Take flamenco, the dance of the gypsies of southern Spain, for example. Like all gypsies, they are descended from a people who originated in India. The Eastern flavor of their dance, partly a legacy of India, can probably also be traced to the Moors, whose civilization flourished in Spain until the end of the fifteenth century.

The flamenco dancer doesn't cover much ground and makes no patterns on it. There is very little jumping and no running or skipping. Instead, there is a complex hammering of the feet, especially the heels, punctuated by the clapping of hands or the clacking of castanets, and accompanied by guitar and, sometimes, a singer. Only the ramrod-straight torso of the dancer is truly in the European tradition — though few other Europeans can match that superbly proud posture.

The underlying meanings of most European dances have been suppressed or forgotten, their movements and gestures stylized beyond recognition, their rough edges smoothed over. But it is probable that many leaping dances, especially those in Slavic countries, are derived from ancient hunting dances imitating animals. The traditional maypole dance, a custom of many English villages, which has also been taken by emigrants to parts of northeastern America, seems to have

links with ancient fertility rituals. The carnival dances of Catholic Europe contain many pagan elements, including impersonations of witches and devils.

All sorts of ancient ritual overtones can be found in the most picturesque of English folk dances, the morris. The dance has regional variations, but typically includes six men dressed in white shirts and trousers, and straw hats, embellished with flowers, ribbons, and bells, plus, often, a man dressed as a woman (Maid Marian), one in a smock (the Fool), and one in hunting coat and top hat with a crude hobbyhorse around his hips. The dancers perform figures, using skipping, kicking, and jumping steps. In some dances they wave handkerchiefs; in others they carry branches of greenery or short sticks which they strike together. This last custom is a feature of dances in many countries of the world; in some cases it derives from mimetic war dances; in others it is a form of percussion to accompany the dance.

The name morris is derived from *moresque*, or Moorish — an aspect reflected in the fact that some morris men blacken their faces. Exactly when and how the dance reached England is not known, but it may have Mediterranean links. To this day, similar dances, called *moriscos*, are performed in parts of Spain, Latin America, and the Middle East. They all seem to be based on celebrating the rebirth of a pagan god and are associated with the renewal of fertility in spring. The exact significance, in the morris, of the hobby-horse man, the Maid Marian figure, and the fool are mysteries that may never be unraveled.

The complex patterns in the morris are an indication that it developed from the "chain" type of dance — originally a simple line of dancers following the leader. The other basic pattern was the ring. These two forms, accompanied by the singing of the dancers themselves, constituted the earliest type of Western European dance, the *carole*. The chain dances tended to develop into dances that made patterns, whereas the simpler circling movement of the ring encouraged dances involving intricate footwork.

The first medieval chain dance was called a *farandole*. It could follow all sorts of patterns, twisting and turning back onto itself. If performed out of doors, it could, of course, travel all through the village, over the fields, wherever the leader chose. The dancers might use a combination of running, skipping, and leaping steps. Sometimes the first two dancers might form an arch, while the rest of the chain passed under it. This arch symbolized a gateway into the next world.

The meandering patterns of the *farandole* gradually became more complex. One variation, called a hey, is found in many British folk dances besides the morris, including Scottish country dancing and the American Virginia reel. In a hey, two lines of dancers move past each other in opposing directions.

The other basic form of medieval *carole* was the *branle*. In this dance the participants might form an arc or a closed circle. The dancers moved mainly in a clockwise direction, but reversed the movement at regular intervals, producing a pendulum-like swaying.

Left *Detail from* The Wedding Dance *by Pieter Breughel the Younger. The picture, painted at the end of the sixteenth century, shows Flemish peasants celebrating a wedding in their traditional lusty style.*

Above *Dances from Eastern Europe combine grace and agility. They demand great strength, especially on the part of the men, who frequently perform tremendous leaps. These Cossack dancers are performing in an Irish street.*

Right *An American square dancing class in Ireland. The dance developed from the French quadrille, which was also in the form of a square and was itself derived from English country dances.*

Several different steps were used in a *branle*, but the two basic steps were the simple and the double. As the drawings show, in a simple branle, one foot moves a short distance to one side and the other then joins it. A double consists of three walking steps in the same direction followed by a pause or by closing the free foot up to the one that made the last step. These basic steps could be combined in many ways. Later, they formed the basis of court dancing, where they might also be danced forward or backward.

While the aristocracy developed these basic forms into ever more elaborate dances, the peasantry enjoyed more vigorous dance — not only as a celebration of festivals but as a temporary escape from the cares and suffering of everyday life. Flemish and German artists painted peasants lustily whirling about in a popular dance called the *hoppaldei*. In this dance, according to one observer, people rushed about "like wild bears" and "as though they wanted to fly."

The history of Western dance is full of examples of folk dance influencing the more refined dance of the ballroom. But there are also examples of influence in the other direction. The Highland Scot's sword dance, with its precise and delicate footwork over a pair of crossed swords on the ground, is related to the French *rigaudon*, a court dance that may have been introduced to Scotland by the royal house of the Stuarts.

Perhaps more surprising is the connection between American square dance and the French quadrille (see page 23). This nineteenth-century ballroom dance was itself derived from earlier English country dances — which probably also crossed the Atlantic in the days of the colonization of North America. But the French influence can be traced in the names of some square dance figures, such as "promenade" and "do-si-do" (*dos à dos*, or "back to back"), in which the man and woman dance forward around each other.

However much it may owe to nineteenth-century ballroom dancing, square dance is emphatically rustic, even when danced today by city dwellers. A distinctive feature of square dancing is the calling of the figures. Besides having a practical advantage, by making it possible for anyone who knows the basic steps to follow any dance without learning it first, the caller's singsong instructions also underscore the rhythm and serve as a humorous patter: "Lady in the lead, Indian-style"; "Dig for the oyster, dive for the clam"; "Anywhere, I don't care, park your lady in a rockin' chair!"

In the past, most folk dance has been rural in origin. Its sources, as we have seen, are to be found in the natural world; in the seasons, the earth and its vegetation, the movements of animals. All this is remote from the city dweller. There are a few examples of what we might call urban folk dance: the Argentine tango came from the slums of Buenos Aires; and the *apache* was a rough dance of the Paris underworld in the early 1900s. In this century, as we shall see, several new forms of social and theatrical dance in the West have sprung from the black neighborhoods of American cities.

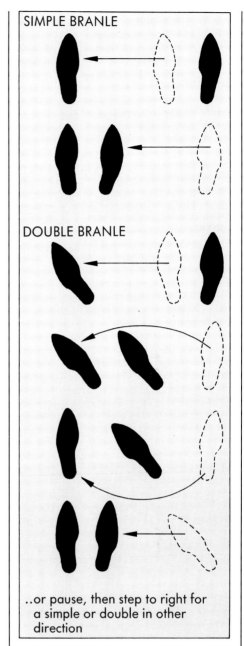

SIMPLE BRANLE

DOUBLE BRANLE

..or pause, then step to right for a simple or double in other direction

This diagram shows the steps of one version of the simple and double branle. *There were possibly other versions, but as there was no way of recording early dance, all we know about it has been handed down from generation to generation.*

4 Social Dance

A hundred years ago it would have been a simple matter to define social dancing — or ballroom dancing, as it could then accurately be called. This was dancing by formally-dressed couples, sometimes individually, sometimes in groups, using established steps and generally accompanied by professional musicians. Most of the dances, including the waltz and the polka, were derived from folk dance, but had been refined to suit the formal surroundings of a ballroom and the tastes and manners of "polite society." Learning how to perform these dances correctly was part of the education of every young lady and gentleman.

Today, except for a few enthusiasts, ballroom dancing has become a somewhat old-fashioned pastime. Elaborate versions are performed in competitions by dancers whose technique is as dazzling as their sequin-spattered costumes. But for most people, social dancing is something completely different. It consists of more or less random rhythmic movements, performed facing, but not touching, one's partner, to the sound of loud music. There is little in the way of steps, and few people take lessons in it.

Inset left *Couples dancing at the home of a nobleman in fifteenth-century Germany.*

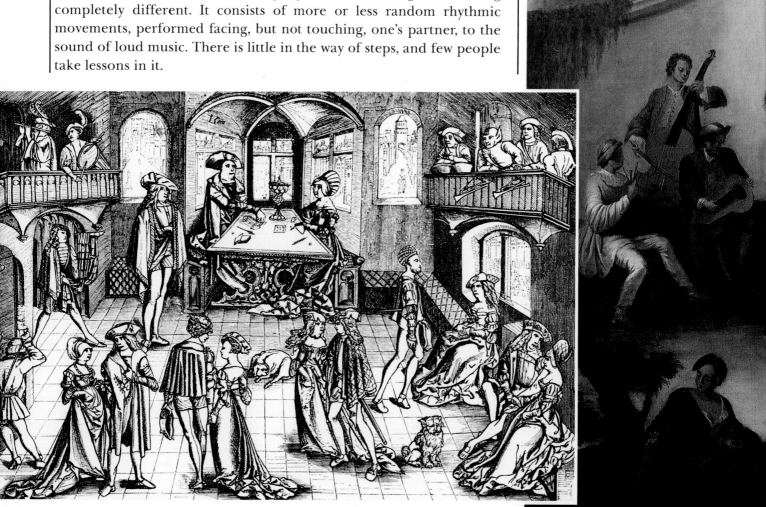

Nothing could be further in spirit from the earliest recognizable form of social dance — performed in the courts of medieval Europe by the aristocracy. The first court dances were basically the simple *branles* and *farandoles* of folk tradition. At court, however, these dances were varied and elaborated.

Then at some point, possibly in twelfth-century Provence, in southern France, people began to dance in couples. We know very little about this early couple dance apart from its name, *estampie*. It may have been a processional dance, or the original *danse à deux* (dance for two), in which an individual couple danced for their own enjoyment but also for the entertainment of the rest of the court. This custom was to continue into the eighteenth century, alongside the other custom of groups of couples dancing simultaneously.

Below *A painting by the eighteenth-century French artist, Philippe Mercier, of elegant people dancing in the countryside.*

Another feature of court dance was that it faced toward the front of the hall, where the person of highest rank sat. The dancers began and ended their dance with a bow or reverence, and their dance was addressed to that person, just as ballet and other theatrical dance today is addressed to the audience.

During the late Middle Ages and the Renaissance, Italy led the way in dance, as in all the arts. Some Italian dances were slow, some fast; some, called *balli*, included several different rhythms, whereas *danzas* had only one rhythm. All these dances had certain basic movements in common. They required a locked knee joint (except when the knee was deliberately bent) and a firmly controlled pelvis. An erect posture, balanced over the instep, not the heel, and a flexible, controlled foot were also essential; for the dances of this time — and for a long time to come — involved subtle raising and lowering of the body, called *movimento*. Another crucial element was the gentle swing of the shoulders in opposition to the movement of the feet, called *maniera*. Arms were normally held slightly away from the body and moved naturally, as we can see in many paintings of the time. Couples held each other by the hand, and each person danced with the same foot, rather than using opposing feet, as must be done in the closed position of modern ballroom dancing.

Above *Queen Elizabeth I of England dancing the* volta *with her court favorite, the Earl of Leicester.*

Italian dance style and dances were adopted throughout Europe. There was great variety in these Renaissance dances. The *pavane*, for example, was slow and stately. The *galliard*, with its fast and showy steps for the man, was especially popular in Elizabethan England. The man performed an intricate sequence of hopping steps while his partner more or less marked time. The energetic *volta* required the man to lift his partner into the air — no easy feat considering the weight of her padded and bejeweled costume.

For the next 200 years French dancing masters set the styles and the rules of court dancing. The distinguishing feature of the French style was turned-out feet. Many elegant dances were developed during this period — perhaps the most elegant being the minuet. This graceful dance involved the performing of complex figures, with the man and woman circling around each other, and it was performed to stately, yet lilting music.

Toward the end of the eighteenth century, refined forms of the English country dances made their way across the English Channel. These were danced in square sets of four couples. The French, in turn, invented a new version, the quadrille, which was to remain popular in both Europe and the United States throughout most of the nineteenth century.

Just as the French Revolution swept away the Old Régime, so the aristocratic court dances of the eighteenth century were swept away in the early 1800s by that shocking German upstart, the waltz. Shocking because couples now danced in a semi-embrace, to the horror of the guardians of morality. But there was no stopping the waltz; its giddy, whirling movement perfectly expressed the new spirit of freedom in the air. It became the most popular dance of the nineteenth century, and paved the way for other lively peasant-derived dances such as the polka and mazurka.

Above *This illustration of a French waltz of the early 1900s conveys the whirling movements that made the waltz an instant success when it was first introduced a century earlier.*

Left *A contemporary artist's impression of the Charleston, a fast, rhythmic dance of the 1920s, characterized by kicking and twisting the legs from below the knees.*

23

Right Rock 'n' roll, the dance craze of the 1950s and 1960s, was, and still is, danced to music that grew out of rhythm and blues. It is similar in style to the earlier jitterbug or lindy hop.

Right The sophisticated, intricate steps of the tango are derived from a dance first performed in run-down areas of Argentina.

The waltz was still going strong well into the twentieth century, as new dances, based first on ragtime and jazz, then on swing and Latin American rhythms, took the floor in ballrooms, dance halls, and nightclubs. Many of the early twentieth-century dances, such as the turkey trot and the bunny hug, were based (loosely) on animal movements. It seems likely, however, that the foxtrot got its name from a music hall entertainer, Harry Fox, who introduced a jerky form of the dance in 1914. Eventually it split into two forms, the quickstep and the slow foxtrot.

The Charleston symbolized the giddy spirit of the 1920s. A bouncy dance, it involved swiveling footwork and kicks to front and side, in the latter case often with the knees pressed close together. For a more romantic mood, couples danced the tango. Born in the run-down neighborhoods of Buenos Aires, the tango underwent considerable polishing, but it remains the most erotic of the various Latin American dances popular in Europe and North America in the first half of the twentieth century. Of these, however, the rumba was probably the most popular. Its basic step is a simple box, which was widely used as an all-purpose step earlier in the twentieth century. But the rumba's performance entails a weight shift on each step which gives the hips the swaying movement typical of Latin dancing — and completely foreign to the European tradition of keeping the torso straight at all times.

The influence of black dance, too, brought a new freedom of movement to the dance floor. The lindy hop and jitterbug, both of black American origin, had couples jumping and gyrating around each other during the 1930s and 1940s. Scarcely had the older generation come to terms with the jitterbug when the even raunchier rock 'n' roll, with its provocative pelvic movements, burst onto the scene, changing popular dance drastically.

Then in 1961 the twist arrived. Couples now danced at, rather than with, each other — as radical a change as the waltz had been 150 years earlier. Since the twist, social dancing has been essentially a matter of self-expression. It is worlds away from the disciplined, intricate, subtle movements that once graced the courts of Europe, and close in spirit to the instinctive celebration of the body that gave rise to dance in the first place.

Above *Irene Castle, who, together with her husband Vernon, formed the most popular and accomplished ballroom dancing partnership of the early 1900s.*

5 Ballet

Today ballet is more popular than ever before. Performances by major ballet companies are often sold out, sometimes weeks before they take place. The leading dancers are glamorous figures with thousands of fans; many girls, and a growing number of boys, attend ballet classes.

And yet ballet, originally, was an elite art form — seen only at the royal courts of Europe. In fact, it was performed by the nobility and royalty themselves, talented amateurs who had a dancing lesson every day, as professionals do now. Over the course of 300 years, ballet has changed greatly, becoming much more demanding and athletic. But in a sense it is still an aristocratic art — disciplined, refined, and imbued with a sense of the potential nobility of the human body.

The first ballets formed part of spectacular entertainments devised for the courts of Italian city-states in the sixteenth century. The word "ballet" comes from the Italian *ballare*, "to dance." Along with dancing, these pageants featured mime and poetry and thus gave birth to opera as well as ballet. (Most operas, in fact, include a ballet — a tradition continued up until the early years of this century.) Although usually based on ancient legends of Greek and Roman gods and heroes, early ballets made almost no attempt at historical realism; costumes were heavy and cumbersome, like those worn by the audience, and the steps were basically those performed by the courtiers in their social dancing, but arranged in more complex patterns.

Ballet soon crossed the Italian frontier and spread to other countries. It was especially fashionable at the court of King Louis XIV of France, who was himself a very good dancer. He founded the first school of ballet, the Académie Royale de Danse, in Paris in 1661. Its purpose was to establish correct techniques and raise the art of dance to the highest possible level. Thus ballet acquired the French vocabulary it still uses: *plié* (a bending of the knees), *pas* (step), *jeté* (a leap), and dozens of other terms. More important, it adopted the postures and positions considered most beautiful and harmonious by the French nobility: the turned-out foot, the five basic positions of the feet, the graceful carriage of the arms (partly based on movements used in fencing — another necessary accomplishment of the male courtier) and, above all, a long, elegant line.

A French dancing master of the time stated that dance movements should be performed with "a certain negligence," as though they were perfectly natural; and this is how ballet does look when it is performed by great dancers. But as anyone knows who has ever studied ballet, it is anything *but* natural; and achieving this "negligence" is the result of countless hours of struggle and pain.

Soon after its founding, the Académie merged with the Académie Royale de Musique to become the Paris Opéra. Ballet companies were also established in many other European capitals, and their performances attracted a large public following. Technique continued to improve, as dancers vied with each other to achieve more dazzling effects. A French ballerina called Camargo was famed for her jumps and credited with having perfected the *entrechat six*, a jump in which the feet are crossed six times in the air. She shortened her costume to mid-calf length (considered very shocking) to display her legs and feet and is said to have removed the heels from her slippers to perform quick footwork more easily.

Artistically, ballet benefited in the mid-1700s from the reforms of Jean-Georges Noverre. A dancer, teacher, and choreographer, he objected to the type of ballet then popular. This consisted of a string of dances with no dramatic or emotional content. But Noverre insisted that ballet should tell a story and "speak to the soul through the eyes." He also objected to heavy, constricting costumes, which impeded movement.

Left *Irek Mukhamledev is one of the top young stars of the Bolshoi Ballet. Russian ballet companies have a long-established tradition of brilliant, vigorous male dancing.*

Below *English ballerina Margot Fonteyn and Rudolf Nureyev, star of the Kirov Ballet who defected from Russia in 1961, dancing in the ballet* Romeo and Juliet. *During their famous partnership at the Royal Ballet in the 1960s and 1970s, they performed many of the great classical roles.*

Noverre's ideas were adopted by many ballet companies, and by the beginning of the nineteenth century it was usual for all ballets to tell a story. Like all the arts, ballet was influenced by the Romantic movement of the early 1800s, which included a fascination with European folklore and with nature. This trend was demonstrated in the ballet *La Sylphide*, in which the hero rejects his earthly sweetheart to pursue an imaginary, idealized vision of womanhood, with tragic results. For the remainder of the century ballet was to be dominated by ethereal creatures in billowy white skirts and, often, little wings or feathers to indicate a supernatural aspect.

The star of the original *La Sylphide* in 1832, Marie Taglioni, was one of the first ballerinas to dance on the tips of her toes — what is called *en pointe*. Shoes were not yet blocked as they are today; the only support was heavy darning at the toe and tightly wrapped ribbons around the ankle, so steps *en pointe* were limited. But the heightened effect of weightlessness thus achieved led to the development of the stiffened shoe and revolutionized ballet technique, at least for women dancers.

Increasingly, ballet was becoming an all-female form of entertainment. Male dancers were given little to do except support the

Above *Vaslev Nijinsky (1890-1950) trained at the Imperial School in St. Petersburg and became the leading dancer in Diaghilev's* Ballet Russe. *He is remembered as one of the greatest dancers of all time, especially noted for his grace and his tremendous leaps.*

Right *Marie Taglioni (1804-84) is known to have danced with astonishing grace. She triumphed with her creation of* La Sylphide *in 1832, which marked the beginning of the romantic era of ballet. She was one of the first ballerinas to dance* en pointe *(on the tips of the toes). She ended her career teaching dancing to the children of Queen Victoria.*

Below *Dancers of the Sadlers Wells Royal Ballet in a performance of* Paquita, *in 1987.*

ballerina, and toward the end of the 1800s men's roles were often danced by women in tights. But exceptions to this decline could be found in Denmark and Russia. The Royal Danish Ballet continued the tradition, established by their great choreographer Auguste Bournonville, of a refined, lyrical style and of strong roles for men. In St. Petersburg (now Leningrad) the Imperial Russian Ballet, founded in 1738, continued to flourish under the direction of the Frenchman Marius Petipa, who created some of ballet's most enduring masterpieces, including *The Sleeping Beauty* and *Swan Lake*, both to music by Tchaikovsky.

It was the Russians who revived ballet in the West. The legendary Anna Pavlova, a dancer of the Imperial Ballet, toured the world between 1905 and 1931, winning new audiences for ballet and causing a sensation wherever she went. The fluidity of her dancing, displayed most memorably in *The Dying Swan*, has never been equaled.

Sergei Diaghilev was neither a dancer nor a choreographer. But he was the manager and the guiding spirit of the company that many believe brought ballet to its full maturity as an art form: the *Ballet Russe*. This troupe of expatriate Russians, based in Monte Carlo, existed a mere twenty years, but in that time it included in its repertoire many of the most brilliant ballets. The troupe's choreographers, Michel Fokine, Léonide Massine, and the young George Balanchine, among others, collaborated with such composers as Rimsky-Korsakov and Stravinsky, and painters such as Matisse and Picasso, producing works in which dance, music, costumes, and scenery perfectly complemented each other. Among the many great ballets commissioned by Diaghilev are *Petrushka, Scheherazade,* and *The Firebird.*

The artistic standards of the *Ballet Russe* were later carried to other countries, and its members founded companies of their own. Among these were George Balanchine, in the United States, Marie Rambert and Ninette de Valois, both in Britain. Thanks to the Polish-born Marie Rambert, who founded the company that bears her name, and the Irish-born Ninette de Valois, who founded what became the Royal Ballet, London is now one of the foremost centers for ballet in the world. The Royal Ballet has established a strong reputation for staging full-length classics such as *Giselle* and *The Nutcracker*; and the tradition of the story-ballet has been enriched by the company's major choreographers, Frederick Ashton and Kenneth MacMillan, who have created such favorite ballets as, respectively, *Maguerite & Armand* and *Romeo and Juliet.*

Below *Members of the Ballet Rambert (now known as the Rambert Dance Company) in their production of* The Rite of Spring. *Originally choreographed by Nijinsky for the* Ballet Russe, *this ballet depicts a ritual human sacrifice in ancient Russia.*

In the United States, George Balanchine founded, in 1948, the New York City Ballet, one of the country's two most important ballet companies — the other being American Ballet Theater. Balanchine's company is famed for the technical brilliance of its dancers, especially the women. As a choreographer, Balanchine excelled in the abstract ballet, in which the dance tells no story but is purely an expression of the music. He created ballets to many different kinds of music, from Bach to the marches of Sousa, and, like Fokine, collaborated with Stravinsky in several works, including the serenely beautiful *Apollo*.

Today, as always, the popularity of ballet is partly due to individual dancers whose technical and artistic genius and sheer star quality have caught the public imagination. But whereas in the past the stars were nearly always the ballerinas, now male dancers have equal — sometimes even top — billing. Alongside the great ballerinas of our time — Margot Fonteyn, Natalia Makarova, Suzanne Farrell and others — we have outstanding male soloists such as Mikhail Baryshnikov and Rudolf Nureyev, who have proved to the public that ballet can be both virile and graceful, powerful and poetic.

A diagram showing the five positions which are the foundation stones of ballet. They were worked out more than 300 years ago by a French dancer and choreographer, Pierre Beauchamp, and were designed to give a dancer perfect balance. Most classical ballet steps start and finish with these five positions.

1st POSITION

2nd POSITION

3rd POSITION

4th POSITIONS

5th POSITION

⑥ Modern Dance

Around the beginning of this century, some dancers began to feel that classical ballet was incapable of expressing the ideas and emotions that they wanted to communicate and had declined into a trivial entertainment. In all the arts there were stirrings of a reaction against the pretty and charming, and a desire to explore the more primitive human emotions. This trend was influenced partly by the work of the psychiatrist Sigmund Freud, who had revealed the inner workings of the subconscious mind.

Artists were also discovering the expressive qualities of arts outside the European tradition. African sculpture, for example, had a strong influence on some European artists. Harmonies and rhythms of Eastern music appeared in the works of some modern composers.

Dance, too, was sensitive to these influences, and while classical ballet began to experience a revival, a new type of dance, known as "modern dance," was born.

The most celebrated pioneer of modern dance was Isadora Duncan. She rejected the discipline of ballet and danced barefoot, in loose, flowing tunics and gowns on a stage devoid of scenery, with only draped curtains as a backdrop. American-born, Duncan was influenced by the landscape of California, where she grew up. She also had an affinity for the culture of ancient Greece and saw, depicted in Greek sculpture, how the human body could be used as an important instrument of expression. Duncan used everyday actions such as walking, running, and swaying in her dances, and gained inspiration from nature as well as from the social and political events of her day. "My art is just an effort to express the truth of my Being in gesture and movement," she wrote in her autobiography. Because her style was so personal and spontaneous, lacking any formal technique, it could not

Above *The American dancer Isadora Duncan (1877-1927). Her interpretive dancing, in flowing draperies and always in bare feet, caused a sensation wherever she danced.*

Left *Mary Wigman and some of her pupils at her school in Germany in the 1920s and early 1930s.*

be taught — although she tried to do so. Many women dancers tried to copy her without success.

Unlike Duncan, who danced to classical music of composers like Schubert and Beethoven, the German dancer Mary Wigman kept music to a minimum, using only percussion instruments such as gongs and wood blocks. Central to her work was the idea of the relationship between the dancer and the surrounding space, which might be imagined as friendly or hostile. She was a great teacher, and pupils from all over the world came to study under her.

Apart from the work of Mary Wigman, almost all of the important work in modern dance before World War II (1939-45) was developed in the United States. Ruth St. Denis found her inspiration in the dances of India and other Eastern countries, which had, she felt, a spiritual quality lacking in Western dance. Her dances were not authentically Oriental, but they opened the public's eyes to the expressive power of Eastern dance movements. Along with the dancer Ted Shawn she founded the Denishawn School of Dance in Los Angeles, which was to produce a great many of the next generation of dance innovators.

The most important of these were Doris Humphrey and Martha Graham. Humphrey's work was characterized by a conflict between the human desire for security, expressed by balance, and the need to take risks and achieve goals, expressed through imbalance.

Above *Dancers of the Martha Graham Dance Company in a performance of one of her ballets, on a theme from a classical legend,* Night Journey.

Left *Dancers of the Ballet Rambert in a performance of* Pierrot Lunaire *by the American choreographer Glen Tetley. This English company was founded in 1931 by Dame Marie Rambert (1888-1982), who worked with Diaghilev but spent most of her life teaching and choreographing.*

Now in her eighties and still teaching, Martha Graham is generally considered the greatest American choreographer of modern dance. Many of her dances are based on classical legends, or on aspects of American history, such as the lives of pioneers depicted in *Appalachian Spring* to hauntingly beautiful music by Aaron Copland. But Graham interprets these stories in twentieth-century terms, focusing on the feelings of the individuals involved and, as she says, "making visible the interior landscape."

To convey the whole range of human emotions, Graham has invented a new vocabulary of dance. She bases these dance movements on the act of breathing: the body expands while inhaling, and contracts while exhaling. The contraction might take the form of a turn, a leap or a fall to the ground. The use of falls and the acknowledgment of the ground are central to Graham's work and to that of most other schools of modern dance. Where classical ballet strives to suggest weightlessness, modern dance never lets the audience forget that humans are creatures of the earth and dependent upon it. And whereas ballet tries to make everything look effortless, Graham's movements suggest the effort required to achieve them. However, the movements are economical; everything, she declares, must be pared down to its essential simplicity. The result is dance of great power and, often, lyrical beauty.

During its first few decades, most modern dance was uncompromisingly stark. Dancers wore black leotards or plain jersey dresses (no shoes), and danced on a bare stage. One reason for this was lack of funds, but many also felt that the dance itself should be allowed to speak directly to the audience without the distractions of costumes and scenery.

Today there has been a relaxation of this purist attitude. The leotard is still the favored costume, because it does not conceal the line of the body. But it is often colored — color is, after all, a powerful conveyor of mood and even ideas.

The new generation of modern dance choreographers also liberally borrow from other dance traditions — folk dance, social dance, even classical ballet. In the work of Paul Taylor, Alvin Ailey, Merce Cunningham and others, a ballet step such as a *développé* (a graceful unfolding of one leg) may be followed by a frantic contraction; moments of serenity can alternate with scenes of great agitation. The work of a single choreographer can include startling contrasts. For example, in *Roses* (1985), Paul Taylor showed romantic love at its most tender, to lyrical music by Wagner. In the same year, he produced *Last Look*, a bleak vision of people apparently in the grip of some horrible illness — jerking convulsively, plucking at their clothing, and staring at themselves in mirrors, as if to prove that they exist.

In such works as these, modern choreographers are remaining true to the aims of the early twentieth-century innovators: to portray all aspects of the human condition using those movements that seem most natural and appropriate.

Above *The Merce Cunningham Dance Company performing in 1987 at the annual Spoleto dance festival held in Charleston, South Carolina.*

Along with classical ballet and modern dance, many other forms of theatrical dance have long enjoyed a huge popular following. In the nineteenth century, variety shows — known as vaudeville in the United States and music hall in Britain — featured groups of pretty girls in graceful, ballet-derived movements which involved much waving of their long, full skirts. The French took the same basic idea and transformed it into the high-kicking, high-spirited cancan that became a regular feature of the French review.

Another attraction of vaudeville was tap dancing. A fusion of several folk traditions, including the English clog dance, the Irish jig, and the foot-stamping dances of Africa, tap was originally developed by black Americans. They combined the free body movements characteristic of black dance with the intricate footwork typical of Irish dance, in particular, to create a new form overflowing with vitality.

Originally tap was mainly a dance for men — either a duet or a solo number. Later, tap steps were adapted into dance routines for choruses of girl dancers, such as the famous Bluebell Girls of the *Folies Bergères* and the Radio City Rockettes. And some individual women tap dancers — notably Eleanor Powell and Ann Miller — demonstrated that the liberated modern woman could be as energetic and stylish a "hoofer" as a man.

The development of musical comedy as a distinct form of entertainment in the early twentieth century created new possibilities for dance. The "musical," as it came to be called, was of American origin and was the offspring of operetta and vaudeville. Like operetta, it had a story line; but its music was in the popular styles of vaudeville, especially jazz and the blues. The typical Broadway musical was, and still is, strident and spectacular. It features big dance production numbers which may combine elements of tap, ballroom and/or popular dance, folk dance, and ballet.

In the first few decades of the musical, the dance numbers often had only a remote connection with the story. Then in 1943, the classically-trained dancer and choreographer Agnes DeMille broke new ground with the dances she created for Rodgers' and Hammerstein's *Oklahoma!* Based on ballet, they incorporated movements derived from American frontier life, including cowboys' riding and roping. More importantly, they formed an essential part of the drama, helping to tell the story and develop the characters. In this respect the dances of *Oklahoma!* set a precedent that was to be followed, with few exceptions such as *Cats*, right up to the present day.

Above *The high-kicking cancan, in the form we know it, was performed by chorus girls in French music halls at the end of the nineteenth century.*

Right *Fred Astaire (1899-1987), the incomparable American dancer who revolutionized the movie musical with his original, meticulously worked-out tap dance routines.*

Inset right *The brilliant Gene Kelly performing his celebrated "Singin' in the Rain" number from the movie of the same name.*

In his choreography for *West Side Story* (1957), Jerome Robbins carried the combining of dance and drama even further. Here, the dance was central to the action, especially in the fight scenes. It emerged as naturally as the dialogue and evoked the passions of New York street life as strongly as did Bernstein's music. Robbins later repeated his Broadway success with the more extravagant choreography for the film version of *West Side Story*.

Millions of people who have never seen a stage musical have enjoyed dance in the movies. When sound was added to cinema back in 1927, the opportunities for filming song and dance were instantly apparent; in fact, the very first "talkie," *The Jazz Singer*, was a musical. But it took several more years for directors to learn how to film dance, taking advantage of the special qualities of the medium. By zooming in on dancers the camera could make the viewer feel more involved in the dance, compensating for the loss of the excitement of a live performance. Also, the enormous sets and skillful use of different camera angles and film editing opened up dance, giving it new dimensions. All kinds of fantasy effects became possible.

These possibilities were used to their fullest potential by the director Busby Berkeley. In films such as *Gold Diggers of 1935* and *42nd Street*, he devised spectacular numbers featuring dozens of girls filmed from above while forming elaborate patterns like some giant human kaleidoscope.

Fascinating as they are, such visual tricks are ultimately less satisfying than watching a truly great dancer perform. Of the many fine dancers that were brought to the screen during the great days of the Hollywood musical, two stand out above all the others: Gene Kelly and the late Fred Astaire.

"Elegant" is the word most often used to describe Astaire, who is most fondly remembered in white tie and tails, nimbly and gracefully

Below left *A scene from* Fame, *a musical drama set against the background of Fiorello La Guardia High School of Performing Arts.*

Below *Fred Astaire and Ginger Rogers, the greatest of all Hollywood partnerships, in a scene from* The Gay Divorcee, *one of Hollywood's lavish musicals of the 1930s.*

Above *A scene from the popular stage musical* Cats, *with songs and music by Andrew Lloyd Webber, and choreography by Gillian Lynne.*

whirling over a polished ballroom floor with his perfectly matched partner Ginger Rogers. Astaire was a virtuoso tap dancer, noted especially for his "broken rhythm," a technique of dancing first on the beat, then off it, then back on it again. He was also a great innovator, always on the lookout for new ideas. One of his solos in *Shall We Dance*, set in an immaculate ship's engine room, was originally inspired by the rhythm of a cement mixer.

In contrast to Astaire's cool, somewhat detached style, with its dazzling footwork, Gene Kelly was more relaxed and athletic, more influenced by ballet, and more emotionally involved. The title song from *Singin' in the Rain* — probably the most famous of all film dance numbers — shows Kelly at his best. The joyous exuberance of it is infectious: audience members feel as though they too are dancing.

Kelly's gifts as a choreographer were best displayed, however, in *An American in Paris*. Studded with charming dances set to music by George Gershwin, the film ends with Kelly's version of the "American in Paris" ballet, a brilliant fusion of dance styles ranging from classical ballet to jitterbug.

The golden age of the Hollywood musical ended thirty years ago. But outstanding musicals are still being made, if not in quite such rapid succession. Such box office hits as *Fame, A Chorus Line*, and *Saturday Night Fever* have proved that dance on film continues to be as captivating as ever.

8 Dance Today

"Gotta dance! Gotta dance!" sang Gene Kelly as a stage-struck young hoofer in the *Singin' in the Rain* Broadway episode. It's a sentiment many people today share, even if they have no stage ambitions.

Some, of course, simply dance for fun, or also — in the case of folk dance — to explore an old tradition of their own, or another culture. But for most, perhaps, the main reason is health. In this health-conscious age, everyone is aware of the importance of taking exercise of some kind, and one of the best and most pleasant ways of keeping fit is by dancing.

There's a type of dance to suit every taste and physique: tap, ballet, modern and all kinds of folk dance, from square dance to flamenco. But one of the most popular is jazz dance.

Defining jazz dance is not easy. In terms of its steps and movements it is wide-ranging, containing movements related to disco dance, ballet, modern dance, and Caribbean dance, with plenty of scope for improvising. Jazz dance first emerged in the musicals of the 1940s and 1950s, but much of its basic "feel" goes back to African dance. In the *Pineapple Dance Book*, jazz dance is described as coming "from the stomach." The dancer must "feel the movement starting in the stomach, then passing through the rest of the body like a wave . . ."

Among the most basic and characteristic techniques of jazz dance are isolations. These are movements of a single part of the body while the rest of the body remains still. The jazz dancer must learn to isolate not only the arms and legs but also the head, shoulders, chest, and pelvis. Then he or she must also learn polycentrics, in which two or more isolations are performed at the same time — basically the same idea as patting your head and rubbing your stomach simultaneously, though considerably more complex and attractive!

The twisting and shaking movements in jazz dance resemble disco dance, while the tensing and relaxing of the body show the influence of modern dance. The modern dance influence is also seen in the various falls and movements done from a sitting, crouching, or prone position. Still other movements, especially the lively jumps and kicks, are derived from Broadway musical choreography, which, in turn, owes something to ballet technique. In fact, a knowledge of ballet technique is considered essential for a professional jazz dancer, in spite of the many dissimilarities between the two styles.

In its readiness to include and adapt movements from all sorts of dance traditions, jazz dance is perfectly attuned to the spirit of the times. Even more than tap dancing, jazz dance is a blending of European and African movements — a truly cosmopolitan dance form.

Below *Jazz dancing incorporates many of the movements of disco dancing and Broadway musical choreography, and even some ballet.*

Left *The athletic and strenuous movements of breakdancing require a great deal of coordination.*

But perhaps the most original type of dance on the scene today is breakdancing. A product of the 1970s, born in the black neighborhoods of New York City, breakdancing has become a familiar and exciting part of the urban landscape in parts of Europe as well as America. It is as vigorously male as the dance of Cossacks or Masai warriors and every bit as strenuous.

The strong overtones of aggression in breakdancing stem from the fact that it was originally used by street gangs as a way of staking out their territory. Many of the movements convey a message of mockery or threat. Some gangs actually worked out their aggression in breakdance "battles" — which is not so unlikely as it might seem. This dancing requires an enormous amount of energy, so there is not much left over for actual fighting.

Breakdancing requires a high degree of coordination. The whole body is used in rapid combinations of wavelike and snapping or "locking" movements, jumps, and tumbles. Sometimes two or more dancers work together in lightning-fast acrobatic routines, in which the least slip-up in precision could result in a bad injury.

Robotic dance is a dance thoroughly of our time, while owing a lot to long-established Western traditions of mime. The robotic dancer, as the name suggests, imitates a robot imitating a human being. The finely tuned, subtly jerky movements require great concentration and control over individual parts of the body. For the spectator the effect can be somewhat weird.

The expressive power of dance makes it well suited to treating some kinds of emotional illness. Dance therapy of today has its origins in the ritualistic treatment of the ancient shamans. It was first practiced in Europe in the early years of this century. The dance therapist uses a variety of approaches, depending on the problem. For example, a very withdrawn person who has difficulty in expressing feelings may reveal preoccupations or fears through the movements made while dancing to popular music. The therapist can then suggest other movements to widen the patient's range of expression and perhaps foster more positive feelings. Folk dance is sometimes used for its value in helping individuals relate to other people.

For some physical illness, too, dance can be therapeutic. Obviously it improves muscle tone and digestion, and it also helps the circulation. In fact, the founder of the Pineapple Dance Studios in London, Debbie Moore, first started dancing seriously on the advice of her doctor. Some women have found belly dancing helpful during pregnancy, for strengthening the spine and relieving discomfort in the lower back; after childbirth belly dancing also helps to strengthen and restore sagging muscles.

There is also a growing acknowledgment of dance as suitable in religious ritual, after centuries in which the Christian Church regarded it with distrust. Dance in church is still rare, although it plays an important part in the worship of some Christian groups, who emphasize spontaneous, emotional expressions of faith. More formal types of religious dance have been created by a few professional dance companies, including the London Contemporary Dance Theatre, who have performed works to religious music by Beethoven, Vivaldi, and others, in cathedrals and churches. Many amateur dance companies also perform in churches as part of the service and as an act of worship. Such events as these show that the ability of dance to express spiritual feelings has finally been recognized.

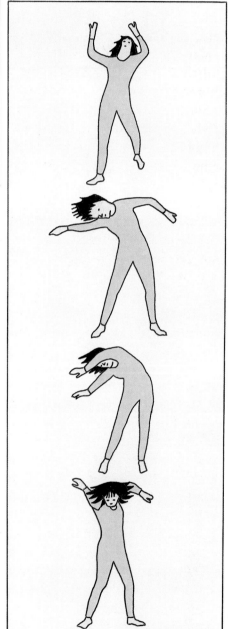

Above *Jazz dance involves many free arm movements, including swings and spirals over the head. These can be soft and flowing or vigorous and dramatic.*

42

9 Creating and Recording a Dance

The art of composing a dance, called choreography, is one of the most complex of all creative processes. The choreographer approaches the task of composing from any one of many starting points: a dramatic idea, such as a story or legend; a piece of music; a feeling or mood; visual material, such as a painting or landscape; a philosophical or political idea; or a pattern of movement, visualized by the choreographer or improvised by the dancers themselves.

Some choreographers use a variety of starting-points for their work. Michel Fokine, the creator of many dances for the *Ballet Russe*, built *Prince Igor* on ancient Tartar dances, using music from the opera of the same name by Borodin. He based his *Paganini* on the life of the great violinist and composer and *Le Spectre de la Rose* on a famous French poem. George Balanchine began with a piece of music, then selected and arranged movements to express the music. Martha Graham begins with an elusive feeling, or "stirring," as she calls it. This seed of an idea may germinate in her mind over a long period while she searches for a way of expressing it. Ninette de Valois used a totally different approach. She would begin by commissioning a complete scenario and music, then work out the choreography within that framework. Working with a pianist, she would plan the steps in detail, before the first rehearsal.

Below *Choreographer Christopher Bruce working with dancers of the Rambert Dance Company.*

This last method is possible if one uses an established dance vocabulary, such as that of classical ballet, although few ballet choreographers work this way. More often, the choreographer (who is almost always a dancer also) tries out steps alone, possibly making a few notes, and then develops these ideas at the rehearsal, using the dancers. If the music is commissioned, the choreographer may work with the composer in the early stages.

The relationship between dance movements and music has often been re-examined in recent years. Traditionally it was assumed that the two must complement each other closely. But many choreographers interpret the idea of "complementary" more freely. Doris Humphrey, for example, would often begin with a piece of music and then develop the movements independently, finally adjusting them to harmonize with the music.

Recently Merce Cunningham has stretched this idea to the limit; he has commissioned music for dances from the avant-garde composer John Cage, merely specifying the length. The dancers do not hear the music until they go on stage for the first performance. There can be no synchronization of movement and music in this method, but the spectator has a choice: to try to relate the music and dance, or to leave them separate.

Some modern choreographers have eliminated music altogether — as Jerome Robbins has done in *Moves* and Twyla Tharp in *The Fugue*. In such works they are exploring the possibility of dance existing on its own terms, as music does.

For many choreographers, the dreaded moment in the creative process is the first rehearsal, for there is usually still a lot of work to be done. The choreographer's job has been compared to writing a play and directing it at the same time. This is especially true in modern dance, where entirely new movements may be created; but even in classical ballet the choreographer must "write" the sequence of steps (although not the steps themselves) while simultaneously coaching the dancers in the nuances of their performances.

Many choreographers are able to remember their completed work in every detail. Others rely on the dancers to remember. Until the twentieth century, in fact, memory was the main method of preserving a dance, which is why so many have been lost. Early dancing masters devised various systems of dance notation, but these were highly individual and not easily understood by others. Also, they were not capable of describing all of the elements of a dance. The development of modern dance, with its profusion of new, un-named movements, has made a universal system of notation even more necessary.

Several such notation systems have now been devised, and two of them, the Laban and the Benesh, are widely used. Video also plays a crucial role in the creation and recording of dance. By videotaping a rehearsal, the choreographer can capture every stage in the development of a dance, every fragment of an idea, and can later study and sift these ideas to evaluate their creative possibilities.

Where to See and Learn Dance

Anyone interested in learning more about dance, either as spectator or performer, should have no difficulty in achieving this goal. In North America today there are a great many dance companies, ranging from internationally famous ballet and modern dance companies to folk ensembles and various small experimental groups. Even if you live in a small town, with no resident company and far off the tour circuit, there is dance on television.

All the major dance companies tour periodically — the arts sections of your local and national newspapers will include listings of performances. Watch out, also, for folk festivals, where you can often see performances of various ethnic dances.

Listed below are some of the major companies that present classical ballet (except where stated otherwise): American Ballet Theater, Australian Ballet Foundation, Bolshoi Ballet, Dance Theater of Harlem, Grand Kabuki (traditional Japanese), Georgian State Dance Company (Russian folk), Kirov Ballet, London Contemporary Dance Theater (modern), London Festival Ballet, Martha Graham Dance Company (modern), Merce Cunningham Dance Company (modern), National Ballet of Canada, New York City Ballet, Paco Peña's Flamenco Dance company (Spanish folk), Rambert Dance Company (modern ballet), Royal Ballet, Royal Danish Ballet, Sadlers Wells Royal Ballet, San Francisco Ballet, Stuttgart Ballet, Twyla Tharp Dance.

Many of these dance companies have an education director, who organizes special programs, lectures, and workshops designed to bring an understanding and appreciation of dance to a wider public, and specifically to schools.

There are many opportunities to learn dance, whether you intend to take it up as a profession or simply to enjoy it as a sparetime activity or for fitness. Anyone intending to become a classical ballet dancer should, ideally, begin training at about the age of six to eight. This is because ballet technique requires a body that has been developed in certain specific ways, and past a certain age it is difficult or impossible to achieve this. Ballet is the most physically demanding of all the arts; and anyone who undertakes it seriously soon learns that success requires not only talent and the right physique but also total commitment and discipline.

You may find that your school offers one or more forms of dance as part of its curriculum. Many schools and colleges offer courses in dance as physical education and fine arts classes. Degrees in dance can also be obtained.

There are other careers in dance besides that of the performing artist. You can train to become a teacher of dance or a dance therapist; and there are careers in dance company management, dance notation, and the keeping of dance archives.

Some of the best-known schools of ballet and modern dance are those attached to the leading dance companies. A few of the well-known schools in the United States are the School of American Ballet (New York City Ballet), the Dance Theater of Harlem school, and the Martha Graham School of Contemporary Dance, all in New York. In Britain there are the Royal Ballet School, the Rambert School of Ballet, and the London Contemporary Dance School, all in London. The National Ballet School of Canada is in Toronto. The Australian Ballet Company is in Melbourne.

There are many opportunities to learn to dance for the fun of it. Check with your local adult education group to see if they offer a suitable dance class for which you might be eligible. Many YMCAs offer courses in dance for children and adults alike. These are less expensive than those offered by private schools. Some private schools of dance such as the Pineapple Dance Studios, in New York and London, have a membership system and charge a small fee when you attend classes. Most dancers begin training at a private dance school. The phone directory gives addresses of local dance teachers.

Classes in folk dance of various kinds are offered by organizations devoted to preserving these folk arts. In the United States the Country Dance and Song Society of America operates an extensive program of classes and other events. In Britain these include the English Folk Dance and Song Society, the Royal Scottish Country Dance Society and the Welsh Folk Dance Society. The Bhavan Institute of Indian Culture, in London, offers classes in Indian Dance.

Finally, if you want to be well informed about dance on a regular basis, you should subscribe to one of the international dance magazines.

Glossary

Avant-garde   Referring to artists whose techniques and ideas are in advance of those generally accepted.

Choreographer   The composer of dance steps and sequences for ballet and stage dancing.

Complement   To relate to something else in such a way as to make a pleasing whole or balance.

Cultural imperialism   The imposing of one country's culture and attitudes upon another country.

Expatriates   People who are exiled or banished from their native country.

Fertility   The state of being fertile, or capable of bringing forth new life.

Figure   A specified set of movements in a dance.

Hoofer   A slang word for a professional dancer, particularly a tap dancer.

Improvise   To make something up as one goes along, without any advance preparation.

Innovator   A person who introduces new methods, techniques, or styles.

Kaleidoscope   A pattern of frequently changing shapes and colors.

Medium   A particular form of artistic expression or means of communication, such as oil painting, film, or dance (plural, media).

Mime   A form of theater in which all the action is expressed physically, without speaking.

Mimetic   Involving imitation.

Notation   A system of signs or symbols used to represent elements, as in music or dance.

Nuance   A subtle variation, gradation, or shade of meaning.

Operetta   A light-hearted or comic type of opera.

Percussion   The striking of musical instruments to produce a sound.

Purist   Describing an attitude that favors keeping the traditional, correct forms, without any alteration or adaptation; or a person who holds this attitude.

Ragtime   A style of jazz music developed around 1900.

Repertoire   The entire collection of dances (or music or plays) that an individual performer or company knows and can perform; also called "repertory."

Scenario   The story line of a dance, or other dramatic or literary work.

Secular   Not concerned with or related to religion.

Slavic   Relating to peoples of eastern Europe and parts of Soviet Asia, such as Bulgaria, Yugoslavia, Poland, Czechoslovakia, Russia.

Solstice   The longest day of summer or the shortest day of winter.

Strathspey   A slow Scottish dance with gliding steps.

Swing   Jazz-based big-band dance music originating in the 1930s.

Virtuoso   Having great technical ability; or a person who has this ability.

Vocabulary   In dance, the whole range of movements.

Further Reading

American Ballet Theatre by Charles Payne (Alfred A. Knopf, 1978).

Baryshnikov at Work by Mikhail Baryshnikov (Alfred A. Knopf, 1976).

The Dance Makers by Elinor Rogosin (Walker, 1980).

The Dance and the Dancer by Merce Cunningham (Scribner Books, 1984).

Dancing for Balanchine by Merril Ashley (E.P. Dutton, Inc., 1984).

The Encyclopedia of Dance and Ballet edited by Mary Clarke and David Vaughn (G.P. Putnam's Sons, 1977).

The Great Russian Dancers by Gennady Smakov (Alfred A. Knopf, 1984).

Movement and Metaphor — Four Centuries of Ballet by Lincoln Kirstein (Praeger Publishers, 1970).

The New York City Ballet by Lincoln Kirstein (Alfred A. Knopf, 1973).

Prime Movers: The Makers of Modern Dance in America by Joseph H. Mazo (William Morrow, 1977).

The Shapes of Change: Images of American Dance by Marcia B. Siegel (Avon Books, 1981).

That's Dancing: A Glorious Celebration of Dance in the Hollywood Musical by Tony Thomas (Harry N. Abrams, 1985).

Winter Season. A Dancer's Journal by Toni Bentley (Random House, 1982).

Index

Picture Acknowledgments

Alexander, Bryan and Cherry 4 (top), 6 (top), 8–9 (lower); Aquarius 37 (top), 38 (left); BBC Hulton 25 (top), 29 (top); Bridgeman Art Library 16, 21; J Allan Cash 10 (top), 15 (both), Chapel Studios 28–9; Bruce Coleman 9; Donald Cooper 39; David Cumming 10 (lower); Mary Evans 20, 23 (top) 36; Michael Holford 12, 12–13; Geoff Howard 31; Camilla Jessell 6–7; Billie Love 11; Mansell Collection 23 (lower), 28 (top); Novosti 26 (top); Photri 30 (top), 34 (top), 36; Popperfoto 24 (top), 33 (both), 38 (left); Ronald Sheridan 12 (lower); Syndication International 5, 18 (both), 40; Topham Picture Library cover, 14, 26–7, 30 (lower), 34 (lower); Wayland Picture Library 4 (lower), 7 (top), 22, 24 (lower), 42 (top); Artwork on pages 19, 32, 42 by Malcolm Walker.